PHOTOGRAPHY
Quail Studio

ART DIRECTION & STYLING
Georgina Brant

DESIGN LAYOUT
Quail Studio

MODEL
Aleja / Rose

HAIR & MAKEUP
Michelle - Court-on-Camera Creatives

KNITTERS
Judith · Louise · Anita · Rebecca
Sarah · Mariana · Margo ·Rachel
Alison · Beverley · Guilia · Shelia

First published in Great Britain in 2022 by
Quail Publishing Limited
Unit 15, Green Farm, Fritwell, Bicester, Oxfordshire,
OX27 7QU
E-mail: info@quailstudio.co.uk

ISBN: 978-1-8384102-3-0
© Patterns & Design Quail Publishing Limited, 2022
© Quail Publishing Ltd, 2022

Essential
PASTELS

CHANTILLY

PATTERN PAGE 30

VIOLET

PATTERN PAGE 32

OAT

PATTERN PAGE 34

CLOUDY
PATTERN PAGE 36

PEA
PATTERN PAGE 38

SMIRK

PATTERN PAGE 40

PERIWINKLE

PATTERN PAGE 42

BLUSHES

PATTERN PAGE 44

FLORA

PATTERN PAGE 48

PATTERNS

HYACINTH

DESIGNED BY
quail studio

SIZE

To fit bust (cm/in)

71-76	81-86	91-97	102-107	112-117	122-127	132-137	142-147	152-157
28-30	32-34	36-38	40-42	44-46	48-50	52-54	56-58	60-62

Actual bust measurement of garment

92	103	112	123	132	143	152	163	175
36¼	40½	44	48½	52	56¼	59¾	64	68¾

YARN | Summerlite 4 ply (50gm)

6	6	7	7	7	8	8	8	9

(photographed in Blushes 420)

NEEDLES

1 pair 2½mm (no 12/13) (US 1½) needles
2½mm (no 12/13) (US 1½) circular needle no longer than 40 cm

EXTRAS

Stitch holders

TENSION

30 sts and 46 rows to 10 cm / 4 in measured over patt using 2½mm (US 1½) needles.

BACK

Using 2½mm (US 1½) needles cast on 138 [154: 168: 184: 198: 214: 228: 244: 262] sts.
Row 1 (RS): P1 [3: 1: 3: 1: 3: 1: 3: 3], K1, *P2, K1, rep from * to last 1 [3: 1: 3: 1: 3: 1: 3: 3] sts, P1 [3: 1: 3: 1: 3: 1: 3: 3].
Row 2 (WS): K1 [3: 1: 3: 1: 3: 1: 3: 3], P1, *K2, P1, rep from * to last 1 [3: 1: 3: 1: 3: 1: 3: 3] sts, K1 [3: 1: 3: 1: 3: 1: 3: 3].
These 2 rows form rib.
Work in rib for a further 4 rows, ending with RS facing for next row.
Now work in patt as folls:
Row 1 (RS): P1 [3: 1: 3: 1: 3: 1: 3: 3], slip next st with yarn at back (WS) of work, *P2, slip next st with yarn at back (WS) of work, rep from * to last 1 [3: 1: 3: 1: 3: 1: 3: 3] sts, P1 [3: 1: 3: 1: 3: 1: 3: 3].
Row 2 (WS): K1 [3: 1: 3: 1: 3: 1: 3: 3], P1, *K2, P1, rep from * to last 1 [3: 1: 3: 1: 3: 1: 3: 3] sts, K1 [3: 1: 3: 1: 3: 1: 3: 3].
These 2 rows form patt.
Cont in patt until back meas 50 [52: 54: 56: 58: 60: 61: 63: 64] cm, ending with RS facing for next row.
Shape shoulders
Keeping patt correct throughout, cast off 5 [6: 7: 7: 8: 9: 10: 11: 12] sts at beg of next 10 [12: 14: 2: 4: 6: 8: 8: 6] rows, then 6 [7: 8: 8: 9: 10: 11: 12: 13] sts at beg of foll 6 [4: 2: 14: 12: 10: 8: 8: 10] rows.
Break yarn and leave rem 52 [54: 54: 58: 58: 60: 60: 60: 60] sts on a holder (for neckband).

FRONT

Work as given for back until 22 [22: 22: 26: 26: 30: 30: 30: 34] rows less have been worked than on back to beg of shoulder shaping, ending with RS facing for next row.
Shape front neck
Next row (RS): Patt 58 [65: 72: 79: 86: 94: 101: 109: 119] sts and turn, leaving rem sts on a holder.
Work each side of neck separately.
Keeping patt correct throughout, dec 1 st at neck edge of next 8 rows, then on foll 5 alt rows, then on 0 [0: 0: 1: 1: 2: 2: 2: 3] foll 4th rows. 45 [52: 59: 65: 72: 79: 86: 94: 103] sts.
Work 3 rows, ending with RS facing for next row.
Shape shoulder
Keeping patt correct throughout, cast off 5 [6: 7: 7: 8: 9: 10: 11: 12] sts at beg of next and foll 4 [5: 6: 0: 1: 2: 3: 3: 2] alt rows, then 6 [7: -: 8: 9: 10: 11: 12: 13] sts at beg of foll 2 [1: -: 6: 5: 4: 3: 3: 4] alt rows **and at same time** dec 1 st at neck edge of next and foll 6th row.
Work 1 row.
Cast off rem 6 [7: 8: 8: 9: 10: 11: 12: 13] sts.
Return to sts left on holder and slip centre 22 [24: 24: 26: 26: 26: 26: 26: 24] sts onto another holder (for neckband). Rejoin yarn with RS facing and patt to end. Complete to match first side, reversing shapings.

SLEEVES

Using 2½mm (US 1½) needles cast on 102 [108: 116: 126: 134: 144: 150: 156: 162] sts.

Row 1 (RS): P1 [1: 2: 1: 2: 1: 1: 1: 1], K1, *P2, K1, rep from * to last 1 [1: 2: 1: 2: 1: 1: 1: 1] sts, P1 [1: 2: 1: 2: 1: 1: 1: 1].

Row 2 (WS): K1 [1: 2: 1: 2: 1: 1: 1: 1], P1, *K2, P1, rep from * to last 1 [1: 2: 1: 2: 1: 1: 1: 1] sts, K1 [1: 2: 1: 2: 1: 1: 1: 1].

These 2 rows form rib.

Work in rib for a further 4 rows, ending with RS facing for next row.

Now work in patt as folls:

Row 1 (RS): P1 [1: 2: 1: 2: 1: 1: 1: 1], slip next st with yarn at back (WS) of work, *P2, slip next st with yarn at back (WS) of work, rep from * to last 1 [1: 2: 1: 2: 1: 1: 1: 1] sts, P1 [1: 2: 1: 2: 1: 1: 1: 1].

Row 2 (WS): K1 [1: 2: 1: 2: 1: 1: 1: 1], P1, *K2, P1, rep from * to last 1 [1: 2: 1: 2: 1: 1: 1: 1] sts, K1 [1: 2: 1: 2: 1: 1: 1: 1].

These 2 rows form patt.

Cont in patt until sleeve meas 19 [20: 20: 21: 21: 21: 21: 21: 21] cm, ending with RS facing for next row.

Cast off in patt.

MAKING UP

Press as described on the information page.

Join both shoulder seams.

Neckband

With RS facing and using 2½mm (US 1½) circular needle, pick up and knit 26 [27: 27: 30: 30: 35: 35: 35: 39] sts down left side of front neck, then replacing the "slip next st with yarn at back (WS) of work" with "K1" patt across 22 [24: 24: 26: 26: 26: 26: 26: 24] sts on front holder, pick up and knit 26 [27: 27: 30: 30: 35: 35: 35: 39] sts up right side of front neck, then replacing the "slip next st with yarn at back (WS) of work" with "K1" patt across 52 [54: 54: 58: 58: 60: 60: 60: 60] sts on back holder. 126 [132: 132: 144: 144: 156: 156: 156: 162] sts.

Round 1 (RS): P2 [1: 1: 2: 2: 2: 2: 2: 1], K1, *P2, K1, rep from * to last 0 [1: 1: 0: 0: 0: 0: 0: 1] st, P0 [1: 1: 0: 0: 0: 0: 0: 1].

This round forms rib.

Cont in rib until neckband meas 3 cm.

Cast off in rib.

Mark points along side seam edges 18 [19: 20.5: 22: 23.5: 25: 26: 27: 28] cm either side of shoulder seams (to denote base of armhole openings). See information page for finishing instructions, setting in sleeves using the straight cast-off method.

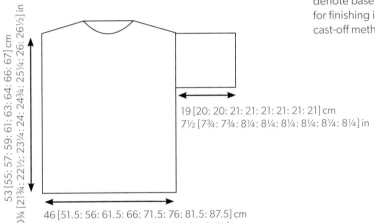

53 [55: 57: 59: 61: 63: 64: 66: 67] cm
20¾ [21¾: 22½: 23¼: 24: 24¾: 25¼: 26: 26½] in

19 [20: 20: 21: 21: 21: 21: 21: 21] cm
7½ [7¾: 7¾: 8¼: 8¼: 8¼: 8¼: 8¼: 8¼] in

46 [51.5: 56: 61.5: 66: 71.5: 76: 81.5: 87.5] cm
18 [20¼: 22: 24¼: 26: 28¼: 30: 32: 34½] in

CHANTILLY

SIZE
To fit bust (cm/in)

71-76	81-86	91-97	102-107	112-117	122-127	132-137	142-147	152-157
28-30	32-34	36-38	40-42	44-46	48-50	52-54	56-58	60-62

Actual bust measurement of garment

81	90	101	110	121	130	141	150	162.5
32	35½	39¾	43¼	47¾	51¼	55½	59	64

YARN | Summerlite DK (50gm)

5	5	5	6	6	7	7	8	8

(photographed in Blushes 480 & White 465)

NEEDLES
1 pair 3¼mm (no 10) (US 3) needles
1 pair 3¾mm (no 9) (US 5) needles
3¼mm (no 10) (US 3) circular needle no shorter than 60 cm long

TENSION
22 sts and 30 rows to 10 cm / 4 in measured over patt using 3¾mm (US 5) needles.

BACK
Using 3¼mm (US 3) needles cast on 89 [99: 111: 121: 133: 143: 155: 165: 179] sts.
Row 1 (RS): K1 [0: 0: 1: 1: 0: 0: 1: 0], *P1, K1, rep from * to last 0 [1: 1: 0: 0: 1: 1: 0: 1] st, P0 [1: 1: 0: 0: 1: 1: 0: 1].
Row 2 (WS): P1 [0: 0: 1: 1: 0: 0: 1: 0], *K1, P1, rep from * to last 0 [1: 1: 0: 0: 1: 1: 0: 1] st, K0 [1: 1: 0: 0: 1: 1: 0: 1].
These 2 rows form rib.
Cont in rib until back meas 6 cm, ending with RS facing for next row.
Change to 3¾mm (US 5) needles.
Now work in patt as folls:
Row 1 (RS): K0 [0: 1: 0: 0: 1: 0: 0: 0], P0 [1: 2: 0: 2: 2: 1: 2: 1], *K2, P2, rep from * to last 1 [2: 0: 1: 3: 0: 2: 3: 2] sts, K1 [2: 0: 1: 2: 0: 2: 2: 2], P0 [0: 0: 0: 1: 0: 0: 1: 0].
Row 2: K0 [0: 0: 0: 1: 0: 0: 1: 0], P1 [2: 0: 1: 2: 0: 2: 2: 2], *K2, P2, rep from * to last 0 [1: 3: 0: 2: 3: 1: 2: 1] sts, K0 [1: 2: 0: 2: 2: 1: 2: 1], P0 [0: 1: 0: 0: 1: 0: 0: 0].
These 2 rows form patt.
Cont in patt until back meas 29 [30: 30.5: 31: 31.5: 32: 32: 33: 33] cm, ending with RS facing for next row.
Place markers at both ends of last row (to denote top of side seams / base of armhole openings).**
Shape armhole and neck slope
Keeping patt correct throughout, cast off 14 [16: 18: 20: 22: 24: 26: 28: 30] sts at beg of **2nd** row, then 10 [11: 12: 13: 14: 15: 16: 17: 18] sts at beg of foll alt row, then 8 sts at beg of next alt row, 6 sts at beg of foll alt row, and 4 sts at beg of next alt row (for neck slope) **and at same time** dec 1 st at armhole edge of next 1 [3: 3: 3: 5: 5: 5: 7: 7] rows, then on foll 3 [2: 3: 3: 2: 2: 2: 1: 1] alt rows, ending with RS facing for next row. 43 [49: 57: 64: 72: 79: 88: 94: 105] sts.
*** Keeping patt correct throughout, dec 1 st at neck slope edge of next 27 [31: 33: 35: 37: 39: 41: 43: 47] rows, then on foll 6 [5: 6: 8: 9: 10: 11: 11: 11] alt rows **and at same time**

dec 0 [0: 0: 1: 1: 1: 1: 1: 1] st at armhole edge of next and foll 0 [0: 0: 0: 0: 1: 2: 2: 3] alt rows. 10 [13: 18: 20: 25: 28: 33: 37: 43] sts.
Cont straight until armhole meas 19 [20: 21.5: 23: 24.5: 26: 27: 28: 29] cm, ending with RS facing for next row.
Shape shoulder
Cast off.

FRONT
Work as given for back to **.
Shape armhole and neck slope
Keeping patt correct, cast off 14 [16: 18: 20: 22: 24: 26: 28: 30] sts at beg of **next** row, then 10 [11: 12: 13: 14: 15: 16: 17: 18] sts at beg of foll alt row, then 8 sts at beg of next alt row, 6 sts at beg of foll alt row, and 4 sts at beg of next alt row (for neck slope) **and at same time** dec 1 st at armhole edge of next 1 [3: 3: 3: 5: 5: 5: 7: 7] rows, then on foll 3 [2: 3: 3: 2: 2: 2: 1: 1] alt rows. 43 [49: 57: 64: 72: 79: 88: 94: 105] sts.
Work 1 row, ending with RS facing for next row.
Complete as given for back from ***.

SLEEVE
Using 3¼mm (US 3) needles cast on 37 [39: 41: 45: 45: 47: 47: 49: 49] sts.
Row 1 (RS): K1, *P1, K1, rep from * to end.
Row 2: P1, *K1, P1, rep from * to end.
These 2 rows form rib.
Cont in rib until sleeve meas 8 cm, ending with **WS** facing for next row.
Next row (WS): P1, inc once in each st to end. 73 [77: 81: 89: 89: 93: 93: 97: 97] sts.

Change to 3¾mm (US 5) needles.
Now work in patt as folls:
Row 1 (RS): *K2, P2, rep from * to last st, K1.
Row 2 (WS): P1, *K2, P2 rep from * to end.
These 2 rows form patt.
Keeping patt correct throughout, inc 1 st at each end of next and every foll 26th [26th: 18th: 28th: 8th: 8th: 6th: 6th: 4th] row to 79 [81: 89: 93: 93: 107: 109: 113: 113] sts, then on every foll – [28th: -: 30th: 10th: 10th: 8th: 8th: 6th] row until there are - [83: -: 95: 103: 109: 113: 117: 123] sts, taking inc sts into patt.
Cont straight until sleeve meas 38 [39: 39: 40: 40: 40: 40: 40: 40] cm, ending with RS facing for next row.
Shape top
Keeping patt correct throughout, cast off 9 [9: 7: 6: 7: 6: 5: 4: 5] sts at beg of next 6 [4: 4: 6: 10: 10: 8: 2: 14] rows, then 0 [10: 8: 7: 0: 7: 6: 5: 6] sts at beg of foll – [2: 4: 4: -: 2: 6: 14: 2] rows.
Cast off rem 25 [27: 29: 31: 33: 35: 37: 39: 41] sts.

MAKING UP
Press as described on the information page.
Join left shoulder seam.
Neckband
With RS facing and using 3¼mm (US 3) circular needle, beg and ending at markers denoting top of right side seam, pick up and knit 42 [45: 48: 51: 54: 57: 60: 63: 66] sts along back slope cast-off edge, 48 [50: 54: 60: 64: 68: 72: 74: 78] sts up back neck slope, 1 st from shoulder seam, 48 [50: 54: 60: 64: 68: 72: 74: 78] sts down front neck slope, and 42 [45: 48: 51: 54: 57: 60: 63: 66] sts along front slope cast-off edge. 181 [191: 205: 223: 237: 251: 265: 275: 289] sts.
Beg with row 2, work in rib as given for sleeve for 6 cm, ending with RS facing for next row.
Cast off in rib.
Join right side seam and neckband seam. See information page for finishing instructions, setting in left sleeve using the set-in method.

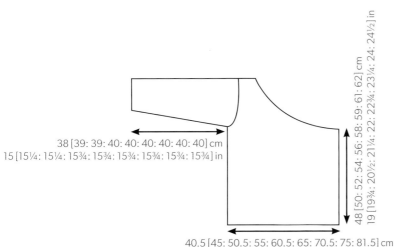

38 [39: 39: 40: 40: 40: 40: 40: 40] cm
15 [15¼: 15¼: 15¾: 15¾: 15¾: 15¾: 15¾: 15¾] in

48 [50: 52: 54: 56: 58: 59: 61: 62] cm
19 [19¾: 20½: 21¼: 22: 22¾: 23¼: 24: 24½] in

40.5 [45: 50.5: 55: 60.5: 65: 70.5: 75: 81.5] cm
16 [17¾: 20: 21¾: 23¾: 25½: 27¾: 29½: 32] in

VIOLET

SIZE

To fit bust (cm/in)

71-76	81-86	91-97	102-107	112-117	122-127	132-137	142-147	152-157
28-30	32-34	36-38	40-42	44-46	48-50	52-54	56-58	60-62

Actual bust measurement of garment

83	93	103	113	123	133	143	153	165
32¾	36½	40½	44½	48½	52¼	56¼	60¼	65

YARN | Kidsilk Haze (25gm)

5	5	5	6	6	6	7	7	8

(photographed in Heavenly 592)

NEEDLES

1 pair 4mm (no 8) (US 6) needles
1 pair 4½mm (no 7) (US 7) needles
4mm (no 8) (US 6) 40 cm long circular needle

EXTRAS

Stitch holders

TENSION

20 sts and 24 rows to 10 cm / 4 in measured over st st using 4½mm (US 7) needles and yarn DOUBLE.

NOTE: yarn is held double THROUGHOUT.

BACK
Using 4mm (US 6) needles and yarn DOUBLE cast on 106 [121: 133: 148: 160: 172: 187: 199: 214] sts.
Row 1 (RS): K3, *P1, K2, rep from * to last st, K1.
Row 2 (WS): K1, *P2, K1, rep from * to end.
These 2 rows form rib.
Work in rib for a further 40 rows, ending with RS facing for next row.
Place markers at both ends of last row (to denote top of side seam openings).
Change to 4½mm (US 7) needles.
Next row (RS): K8 [5: 7: 5: 7: 9: 6: 8: 10], K2tog, (K2, K2tog) 22 [27: 29: 34: 36: 38: 43: 45: 48] times, K8 [6: 8: 5: 7: 9: 7: 9: 10]. 83 [93: 103: 113: 123: 133: 143: 153: 165] sts.
Beg with a **purl** row, now work in st st throughout as folls:
Cont straight until back meas 22 [23: 23.5: 24: 24.5: 25: 25: 26: 26] cm **from markers**, ending with RS facing for next row.
Shape armholes
Place markers at both ends of last row (to denote base of armhole openings).
Work 2 rows, ending with RS facing for next row.
Inc 1 st at each end of next and 8 [7: 5: 3: 2: 0: 0: 0: 0] foll 4th rows, then on 1 [2: 4: 6: 7: 9: 9: 7: 6] foll 6th rows, then on 0 [0: 0: 0: 0: 0: 0: 2: 3] foll 8th rows. 103 [113: 123: 133: 143: 153: 163: 173: 185] sts.
Work 5 [5: 5: 5: 5: 5: 7: 7: 7] rows, ending with RS facing for next row. (Armhole should meas approx 19 [20: 21.5: 23: 24.5: 26: 27: 28: 29] cm.)

Shape shoulders
Cast off 12 [13: 15: 16: 18: 19: 21: 22: 24] sts at beg of next 4 rows, then 11 [13: 14: 16: 17: 19: 20: 23: 25] sts at beg of foll 2 rows.
Break yarn and leave rem 33 [35: 35: 37: 37: 39: 39: 39: 39] sts on a holder (for neckband).

FRONT
Using 4mm (US 6) needles and yarn DOUBLE cast on 106 [121: 133: 148: 160: 172: 187: 199: 214] sts.
Work in rib as given for back for 20 rows, ending with RS facing for next row.
Place markers at both ends of last row (to denote top of side seam openings).
Change to 4½mm (US 7) needles.
Next row (RS): K8 [5: 7: 5: 7: 9: 6: 8: 10], K2tog, (K2, K2tog) 22 [27: 29: 34: 36: 38: 43: 45: 48] times, K8 [6: 8: 5: 7: 9: 7: 9: 10]. 83 [93: 103: 113: 123: 133: 143: 153: 165] sts.
Beg with a **purl** row, now work in st st throughout as folls:
Cont straight until front meas 22 [23: 23.5: 24: 24.5: 25: 25: 26: 26] cm **from markers**, ending with RS facing for next row.
Shape armholes
Place markers at both ends of last row (to denote base of armhole openings).
Work 4 rows, inc 1 st at each end of 3rd of these rows and ending with RS facing for next row. 85 [95: 105: 115: 125: 135: 145: 155: 167] sts.
Divide for front neck
Next row (RS): K42 [47: 52: 57: 62: 67: 72: 77: 83] and turn, leaving rem sts on a holder.
Work each side of neck separately.

Dec 1 st at neck edge of 2nd and foll 12 [13: 11: 11: 10: 10: 9: 7: 6] alt rows, then on 3 [3: 5: 6: 7: 8: 9: 11: 12] foll 4th rows **and at same time** inc 1 st at armhole edge of 3rd [3rd: 3rd: 3rd: 3rd: 5th: 5th: 5th: 5th] and 7 [6: 4: 2: 1: 0: 0: 0: 0] foll 4th rows, then on 1 [2: 4: 6: 7: 8: 8: 6: 5] foll 6th rows, then on 0 [0: 0: 0: 0: 0: 0: 2: 3] foll 8th rows.
35 [39: 44: 48: 53: 57: 62: 67: 73] sts.
Work 3 rows, ending with RS facing for next row.

Shape shoulder
Cast off 12 [13: 15: 16: 18: 19: 21: 22: 24] sts at beg of next and foll alt row.
Work 1 row.
Cast off rem 11 [13: 14: 16: 17: 19: 20: 23: 25] sts.
Return to sts left on holder and slip centre st onto another holder (for neckband). Rejoin yarn with RS facing and K to end. Complete to match first side, reversing shapings.

MAKING UP
Press as described on the information page.
Join both shoulder seams.

Neckband
With RS facing, using 4mm (US 6) circular needle and yarn DOUBLE, pick up and knit 48 [51: 54: 57: 60: 63: 66: 69: 72] sts down left front slope, K st on holder at base of V and mark this st with a coloured thread, pick up and knit 48 [51: 54: 57: 60: 63: 66: 69: 72] sts up right front slope, then work across 33 [35: 35: 37: 37: 39: 39: 39: 39] sts on back holder as folls: K4 [3: 3: 2: 2: 1: 1: 1: 1], inc in next st, (K3, inc in next st) 6 [7: 7: 8: 8: 9: 9: 9: 9] times, K4 [3: 3: 2: 2: 1: 1: 1: 1]. 137 [146: 152: 161: 167: 176: 182: 188: 194] sts.

Round 1 (RS): *K2, P1, rep from * to marked st, K marked st, P1, **K2, P1, rep from ** to end.
This round forms rib.
Keeping rib correct, cont as folls:
Round 2: Rib to within 1 st of marked st, slip next 2 sts as though to K2tog (marked st is second of these 2 sts), K1, pass 2 slipped sts over, rib to end.
Rep last round 7 times more. 121 [130: 136: 145: 151: 160: 166: 172: 178] sts.
Cast off in rib, working dec as set.

Armhole borders (both alike)
With RS facing, using 4mm (US 6) needles and yarn DOUBLE, pick up and knit 91 [97: 103: 112: 115: 124: 127: 136: 139] sts evenly all round armhole edge between markers denoting base of armhole openings.
Row 1 (WS): K1, *P2, K1, rep from * to end.
Row 2: P1, *K2, P1, rep from * to end.
These 2 rows form rib.
Work in rib for a further 5 rows, ending with RS facing for next row.
Cast off in rib.
See information page for finishing instructions, leaving side seams open below markers and noting that, below markers, back is 22 rows longer than front.

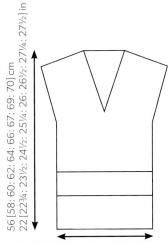

56 [58: 60: 62: 64: 66: 67: 69: 70] cm
22 [22¾: 23½: 24½: 25¼: 26: 26½: 27¼: 27½] in

41.5 [46.5: 51.5: 56.5: 61.5: 66.5: 71.5: 76.5: 82.5] cm
16¼ [18¼: 20¼: 22¼: 24¼: 26¼: 28¼: 30: 32½] in

OAT

SIZE

To fit bust (cm/in)

71-76	81-86	91-97	102-107	112-117	122-127	132-137	142-147	152-157
28-30	32-34	36-38	40-42	44-46	48-50	52-54	56-58	60-62

Actual bust measurement of garment

98	108	119	127	138	148	159	167	180
38½	42½	46¾	50	54¼	58¼	62½	65¼	70¾

YARN | Handknit Cotton (50gm)

11	12	12	13	13	14	14	15	15

(photographed in Blushes 378 & Ecru 251)

NEEDLES

1 pair 4mm (no 8) (US 6) needles

EXTRAS

Stitch holders

TENSION

19 sts and 28 rows to 10 cm / 4 in measured over patt using 4mm (US 6) needles.

BACK

Using 4mm (US 6) needles cast on 92 [104: 113: 122: 131: 140: 152: 158: 170] sts.
Row 1 (RS): K2, *P1, K2, rep from * to end.
Row 2 (WS): P2, *K1, P2, rep from * to end.
These 2 rows form rib.
Work in rib for a further 14 rows, inc [dec: -: dec: -: inc: dec: inc: inc] 1 st at end of last row and ending with RS facing for next row. 93 [103: 113: 121: 131: 141: 151: 159: 171] sts.
Now work in patt as folls:
Row 1 (RS): Knit.
Row 2 (WS): Purl.
Row 3: Knit.
Rows 4 and 5: Purl.
Rows 6 and 7: Knit.
Row 8: Purl.
Rows 9 and 10: As rows 1 and 2.
Row 11: *K2tog, yfwd, rep from * to last st, K1.
Row 12: Purl.
Row 13: K1, *K2tog, yfwd, rep from * to last 2 sts, K2.
Row 14: Purl.
Rows 15 to 18: As rows 11 to 14.
These 18 rows form patt.
Cont in patt until back meas 58 [60: 62: 64: 66: 68: 69: 71: 72] cm, ending with RS facing for next row.
Shape back neck
Next row (RS): Patt 37 [41: 46: 49: 54: 58: 63: 67: 73] sts and turn, leaving rem sts on a holder.
Work each side of neck separately.
Keeping patt correct, dec 1 st at neck edge of next 6 rows. 31 [35: 40: 43: 48: 52: 57: 61: 67] sts.
Work 1 row, ending with RS facing for next row.

Shape shoulder

Cast off.
Return to sts left on holder and slip centre 19 [21: 21: 23: 23: 25: 25: 25: 25] sts onto another holder (for neckband). Rejoin yarn with RS facing and patt to end. Complete to match first side, reversing shapings.

FRONT

Work as given for back until 20 [20: 20: 22: 22: 24: 24: 24: 26] rows less have been worked than on back to **shoulder cast-off**, ending with RS facing for next row.
Shape front neck
Next row (RS): Patt 42 [46: 51: 55: 60: 65: 70: 74: 81] sts and turn, leaving rem sts on a holder.
Work each side of neck separately.
Keeping patt correct, dec 1 st at neck edge of next 8 rows, then on foll 2 [2: 2: 3: 3: 4: 4: 4: 5] alt rows, then on foll 4th row. 31 [35: 40: 43: 48: 52: 57: 61: 67] sts.
Work 3 rows, ending with RS facing for next row.
Shape shoulder
Cast off.
Return to sts left on holder and slip centre 9 [11: 11: 11: 11: 11: 11: 11: 9] sts onto another holder (for neckband). Rejoin yarn with RS facing and patt to end. Complete to match first side, reversing shapings.

SLEEVES

Using 4mm (US 6) needles cast on 41 [41: 44: 47: 47: 47: 47: 50: 50] sts.
Work in rib as given for back for 6 cm, ending with **WS** facing for next row.

Next row (WS): Rib 3 [1: 3: 4: 4: 2: 2: 4: 4], inc in next st, (rib 1, inc in next st) 17 [19: 18: 19: 19: 21: 21: 20: 20] times, rib 3 [1: 4: 4: 4: 2: 2: 5: 5]. 59 [61: 63: 67: 67: 69: 69: 71: 71] sts.

Beg with row 1, now work in patt as given for back, shaping sides by inc 1 st at each end of 27th [21st: 13th: 13th: 9th: 7th: 5th: 5th: 3rd] and every foll 28th [22nd: 14th: 14th: 10th: 8th: 6th: 6th: 4th] row to 63 [69: 71: 73: 85: 89: 83: 93: 77] sts, then on every foll 30th [-: 16th: 16th: -: 10th: 8th: 8th: 6th] row until there are 65 [-: 75: 79: -: 91: 95: 99: 103] sts, taking inc sts into patt.

Cont in patt until sleeve meas 42 [43: 43: 44: 44: 44: 44: 44: 44] cm, ending with RS facing for next row.

Cast off in patt.

MAKING UP
Press as described on the information page.
Join right shoulder seam.

Neckband
With RS facing and using 4mm (US 6) needles, pick up and knit 17 [17: 17: 19: 19: 21: 21: 21: 23] sts down left side of front neck, K across 9 [11: 11: 11: 11: 11: 11: 11: 9] sts on front holder, pick up and knit 17 [17: 17: 19: 19: 21: 21: 21: 23] sts up right side of front neck, and 7 sts down right side of back neck, K across 19 [21: 21: 23: 23: 25: 25: 25: 25] sts on back holder inc 1 [0: 0: 0: 0: 0: 0: 0: 1] st at centre, then pick up and knit 7 sts up left side of back neck. 77 [80: 80: 86: 86: 92: 92: 92: 95] sts.

Beg with row 2, work in rib as given for back for 6 cm, ending with RS facing for next row.

Cast off in rib.

Join left shoulder and neckband seam. Mark points along side seam edges 18 [19: 20.5: 22: 23.5: 25: 26: 27: 28] cm either side of shoulder seams (to denote base of armhole openings). See information page for finishing instructions, setting in sleeves using the straight cast-off method.

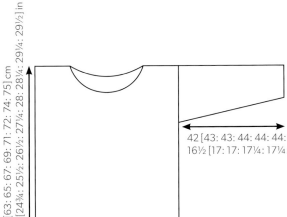

42 [43: 43: 44: 44: 44: 44: 44: 44] cm
16½ [17: 17: 17¼: 17¼: 17¼: 17¼: 17¼: 17¼] in

61 [63: 65: 67: 69: 71: 72: 74: 75] cm
24 [24¾: 25½: 26½: 27¼: 28: 28¼: 29¼: 29½] in

49 [54: 59.5: 63.5: 69: 74: 79.5: 83.5: 90] cm
19¼ [21¼: 23½: 25: 27¼: 29¼: 31¼: 32¾: 35½] in

CLOUDY

SIZE

To fit bust (cm/in)

71-76	81-86	91-97	102-107	112-117	122-127	132-137	142-147	152-157
28-30	32-34	36-38	40-42	44-46	48-50	52-54	56-58	60-62

Actual bust measurement of garment

86	96	106	116	126	136	146	156	167
33¾	37¾	41¾	45¾	49½	53½	57½	61½	66

YARN | Summerlite 4 ply (50gm)

5	5	5	6	6	7	7	7	8

(photographed in Duck Egg 419)

NEEDLES

1 pair 3mm (no 11) (US 2/3) needles
1 pair 3¼mm (no 10) (US 3) needles
3mm (no 11) (US 2/3) circular needle no longer than 40 cm

EXTRAS

Cable needle
Stitch holders

TENSION

32 sts and 36 rows to 10 cm / 4 in measured over patt using 3¼mm (US 3) needles.

SPECIAL ABBREVIATION

C6B = slip next 3 sts onto cable needle and leave at back of work, K3, then K3 from cable needle.

BACK

Using 3mm (US 2/3) needles cast on 105 [115: 127: 141: 151: 163: 177: 187: 201] sts.
Row 1 (RS): K1, *P1, K1, rep from * to end.
Row 2 (WS): P1, *K1, P1, rep from * to end.
These 2 rows form rib.
Work in rib until back meas 10 cm, ending with **WS** facing for next row.
Next row (WS): Rib 6 [2: 4: 6: 2: 4: 6: 2: 5], inc once in each of next 3 sts, *rib 6, inc once in each of next 3 sts, rep from * to last 6 [2: 3: 6: 2: 3: 6: 2: 4] sts, rib 6 [2: 2: 6: 2: 2: 6: 2: 3], (inc in last st) 0 [0: 1: 0: 0: 1: 0: 0: 1] times. 138 [154: 170: 186: 202: 218: 234: 250: 268] sts.
Change to 3¼mm (US 3) needles.
Now work in patt as folls:
Row 1 (RS): P6 [2: 4: 6: 2: 4: 6: 2: 5], K6, *P6, K6, rep from * to last 6 [2: 4: 6: 2: 4: 6: 2: 5] sts, P6 [2: 4: 6: 2: 4: 6: 2: 5].
Row 2: K6 [2: 4: 6: 2: 4: 6: 2: 5], P6, *K6, P6, rep from * to last 6 [2: 4: 6: 2: 4: 6: 2: 5] sts, K6 [2: 4: 6: 2: 4: 6: 2: 5].
Row 3: P6 [2: 4: 6: 2: 4: 6: 2: 5], C6B, *P6, C6B, rep from * to last 6 [2: 4: 6: 2: 4: 6: 2: 5] sts, P6 [2: 4: 6: 2: 4: 6: 2: 5].
Row 4: As row 2.
Rows 5 and 6: As rows 1 and 2.
These 6 rows form patt.
Cont in patt until back meas 21.5 [22.5: 23: 23.5: 24: 24.5: 24.5: 25.5: 25.5] cm, ending with RS facing for next row.

Shape armholes

Keeping patt correct throughout, cast off 6 [8: 9: 10: 11: 12: 14: 16: 17] sts at beg of next 2 rows. 126 [138: 152: 166: 180: 194: 206: 218: 234] sts.**
Dec 1 st each end of next 5 [7: 9: 9: 11: 13: 13: 15: 17] rows, then on foll 5 [7: 8: 9: 11: 11: 13: 15: 17] alt rows, then on foll 4th row. 104 [108: 116: 128: 134: 144: 152: 156: 164] sts.
Cont straight until armhole meas 27 [28: 29.5: 31: 32.5: 34: 35: 36: 37] cm, ending with RS facing for next row.

Shape shoulders

Keeping patt correct throughout, cast off 22 [22: 26: 30: 33: 37: 41: 43: 47] sts at beg of next 2 rows.
Break yarn and leave rem 60 [64: 64: 68: 68: 70: 70: 70: 70] sts on a holder (for neckband).

FRONT

Work as given for back to **.
Dec 1 st at each end of next 5 [7: 9: 9: 11: 13: 13: 15: 17] rows, then on foll 3 [4: 6: 7: 8: 8: 10: 11: 10] alt rows. 110 [116: 122: 134: 142: 152: 160: 166: 180] sts.
Work 1 row, ending with RS facing for next row.

Divide for front neck

Next row (RS): Work 2 tog, patt 53 [56: 59: 65: 69: 74: 78: 81: 88] sts and turn, leaving rem sts on a holder. 54 [57: 60: 66: 70: 75: 79: 82: 89] sts.
Work each side of neck separately.
Keeping patt correct, dec 1 st at neck edge of 2nd and foll 24 [29: 29: 31: 30: 31: 31: 31: 29] alt rows, then on 4 [1: 1: 1: 2: 2: 2: 2: 4] foll 4th rows, then on foll 6th row **and at same time** dec 1 st at armhole edge of 2nd and foll 0 [1: 0: 0: 1: 1: 1: 2: 5] alt rows, then on foll 4th row. 22 [22: 26: 30: 33: 37: 41: 43: 47] sts.
Cont straight until front matches back to shoulder cast-off, ending with RS facing for next row.

Shape shoulder

Cast off.

Return to sts left on holder, rejoin yarn with RS facing and patt to last 2 sts, work 2 tog. 54 [57: 60: 66: 70: 75: 79: 82: 89] sts. Complete to match first side, reversing shapings.

MAKING UP

Press as described on the information page.

Join both shoulder seams.

Neckband

With RS facing and using 3mm (US 2/3) circular needle, pick up and knit 82 [82: 82: 86: 88: 90: 90: 90: 94] sts down left side of front neck, 1 st from base of V neck and mark this st with a coloured thread, and 82 [82: 82: 86: 88: 90: 90: 90: 94] sts up right side of front neck, then patt across 60 [64: 64: 68: 68: 70: 70: 70: 70] sts on back holder as folls: patt 3 [5: 3: 7: 7: 2: 0: 0: 2] sts, (sl 1, K1, psso, P6) 0 [0: 1: 0: 0: 0: 1: 1: 0] times, (K2tog, K2, sl 1, K1, psso, P6) 2 [2: 1: 2: 2: 2: 2: 2: 2] times, (K2tog, K2tog, sl 1, K1, psso) 1 [1: 0: 1: 1: 0: 1: 1: 0] times, (K2tog, K2, sl 1, K1, psso, P2, P2tog, P2, K2tog, K2, sl 1, K1, psso) 0 [0: 1: 0: 0: 1: 0: 0: 1] times, (P6, K2tog, K2, sl 1, K1, psso) 2 [2: 1: 2: 2: 2: 2: 2: 2] times, (P6, K2tog) 0 [0: 1: 0: 0: 0: 1: 1: 0] times, patt 3 [5: 3: 7: 7: 2: 0: 0: 2] sts. 214 [218: 218: 230: 234: 238: 238: 238: 246] sts.

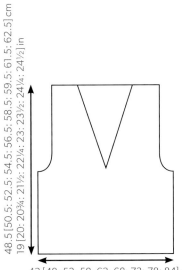

48.5 [50.5: 52.5: 54.5: 56.5: 58.5: 59.5: 61.5: 62.5] cm
19 [20: 20¾: 21½: 22¼: 23: 23½: 24¼: 24½] in

43 [48: 53: 58: 63: 68: 73: 78: 84] cm
17 [19: 20¾: 22¾: 24¾: 26¾: 28¾: 30¾: 33] in

Round 1 (RS): *K1, P1, rep from * to end.

This round forms rib.

Keeping rib correct, cont as folls:

Round 2: Rib to within 1 st of marked st, slip next 2 sts as though to K2tog (marked st is second of these 2 sts), K1, pass 2 slipped sts over, rib to end.

Rep last round 16 times more. 180 [184: 184: 196: 200: 204: 204: 204: 212] sts.

Cast off in rib, decreasing as set.

Armbands

With RS facing and using 3mm (US 2/3) circular needle, pick up and knit 163 [171: 183: 193: 203: 213: 223: 233: 241] sts evenly all round armhole edge.

Beg with row 2, work in rib as given for back, dec 1 st at each end of 2nd and 7 foll 3rd rows. 147 [155: 167: 177: 187: 197: 207: 217: 225] sts.

Work 1 row, ending with RS facing for next row.

Cast off in rib.

See information page for finishing instructions.

PEA

SIZE
To fit bust (cm/in)

71-76	81 86	91-97	102-107	112-117	122-127	132-137	142-147	152-157
28-30	32-34	36-38	40-42	44-46	48-50	52-54	56-58	60-62

Actual bust measurement of garment

	82	92	102	112	122	132	142	152	163
	32¼	36¼	40¼	44	48	52	56	60	64½

YARN | Summerlite DK (50gm)

5	5	5	6	6	6	7	7	7

(photographed in Pear 463)

NEEDLES
1 pair 3¼mm (no 10) (US 3) needles
1 pair 3½mm (no 9/10) (US 4) needles
3¼mm (no 10) (US 3) circular needle no shorter than 60 cm

EXTRAS
Cable needle
Stitch holders

TENSION
28 sts and 32 rows to 10 cm / 4 in measured over g st using 3½mm (US 4) needles.
Cable panel (20 sts) measures 8 cm / 3¼ in.

SPECIAL ABBREVIATIONS
C2B = slip next st onto cable needle and leave at back of work, K1, then K1 from cable needle; **C2F** = slip next st onto cable needle and leave at front of work, K1, then K1 from cable needle; **C4B** = slip next 2 sts onto cable needle and leave at back of work, K2, then K2 from cable needle; **C4F** = slip next 2 sts onto cable needle and leave at front of work, K2, then K2 from cable needle.

CABLE PANEL (20 sts)
Row 1 (RS): P2, C2B, P2, K8, P2, C2F, P2.
Row 2 (WS) and every foll alt row: K2, P2, K2, P8, K2, P2, K2.
Row 3: P2, C2B, P2, C4B, K4, P2, C2F, P2.
Row 5: As row 1.
Row 7: P2, C2B, P2, K4, C4F, P2, C2F, P2.
Row 8: As row 2.
These 8 rows form cable panel.

BACK and FRONT (both alike)
Using 3¼mm (US 3) needles cast on 79 [91: 103: 115: 127: 139: 151: 163: 177] sts.
Row 1 (RS): K1, *P1, K1, rep from * to end.
Row 2 (WS): P1, *K1, P1, rep from * to end.
These 2 rows form rib.
Work in rib until back meas 5 cm, ending with **WS** facing for next row.
Next row (WS): Rib 3 [3: 3: 3: 3: 3: 3: 3: 4], inc in next st, (rib 5, inc in next st) 12 [14: 16: 18: 20: 22: 24: 26: 28] times, rib 3 [3: 3: 3: 3: 3: 3: 3: 4]. 92 [106: 120: 134: 148: 162: 176: 190: 206] sts.

Change to 3½mm (US 4) needles.
Now work in patt, placing cable panels as folls:
Row 1 (RS): K4 [8: 11: 15: 18: 22: 25: 29: 33], work next 20 sts as row 1 of cable panel, (K12 [15: 19: 22: 26: 29: 33: 36: 40], work next 20 sts as row 1 of cable panel) twice, K4 [8: 11: 15: 18: 22: 25: 29: 33].
Row 2 (WS): K4 [8: 11: 15: 18: 22: 25: 29: 33], work next 20 sts as row 2 of cable panel, (K12 [15: 19: 22: 26: 29: 33: 36: 40], work next 20 sts as row 2 of cable panel) twice, K4 [8: 11: 15: 18: 22: 25: 29: 33].
These 2 rows set the sts – 3 cable panels with g st between and at sides.
Keeping patt as set throughout, inc 1 st at each end of 3rd and 7 foll 10th rows, taking inc sts into g st. 108 [122: 136: 150: 164: 178: 192: 206: 222] sts.
Cont straight until work meas 31 [32: 32.5: 33: 33.5: 34: 34: 35: 35] cm, ending with RS facing for next row.
Shape armholes and divide for neck
Next row (RS): Cast off 8 [9: 11: 12: 13: 14: 15: 17: 18] sts, patt until there are 46 [52: 57: 63: 69: 75: 81: 86: 93] sts on right needle and turn, leaving rem sts on a holder.
Work each side of neck separately.
Keeping patt correct, dec 1 st at neck edge of next 4 [6: 4: 4: 2: 4: 4: 2: 2] rows, then on foll 18 [17: 18: 17: 18: 17: 15: 16: 15] alt rows, then on 1 [2: 3: 5: 6: 7: 9: 10: 11] foll 4th rows **and at same time** dec 1 st at armhole edge of 2nd and foll 8 [8: 10: 10: 12: 12: 14: 16: 18] rows, then on foll 7 [10: 11: 12: 12: 14: 15: 16: 18] alt rows, then on foll 4th row. 6 [7: 9: 13: 17: 19: 22: 24: 27] sts.
Cont straight until armhole meas 17 [18: 19.5: 21: 22.5: 24: 25: 26: 27] cm, ending with RS facing for next row.

Shape shoulder
Cast off.
Return to sts left on holder, rejoin yarn with RS facing and patt to end, turn and cast off 8 [9: 11: 12: 13: 14: 15: 17: 18] sts. 46 [52: 57: 63: 69: 75: 81: 86: 93] sts. Complete to match first side, reversing shapings.

MAKING UP
Press as described on the information page.
Join right shoulder seam.
Neckband
With RS facing and using 3¼mm (US 3) circular needle, pick up and knit 54 [58: 62: 68: 72: 76: 80: 84: 86] sts down left side of front neck, place marker on right needle, pick up and knit 54 [58: 62: 68: 72: 76: 80: 84: 86] sts up right side of front neck, and 54 [58: 62: 68: 72: 76: 80: 84: 86] sts down right side of back neck, place second marker on right needle, then pick up and knit 54 [58: 62: 68: 72: 76: 80: 84: 86] sts up left side of back neck.
216 [232: 248: 272: 288: 304: 320: 336: 344] sts.
Cast off knitwise (on **WS**), working "K2tog" at either side of both markers.
Join left shoulder and neckband seam.

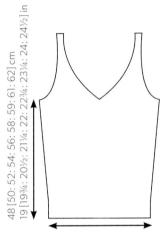

48 [50: 52: 54: 56: 58: 59: 61: 62] cm
19 [19¾: 20½: 21¼: 22: 22¾: 23¼: 24: 24½] in

41 [46: 51: 56: 61: 66: 71: 76: 82] cm
16¼ [18: 20: 22: 24: 26: 28: 30: 32¼] in

Armbands
With RS facing and using 3¼mm (US 3) circular needle, pick up and knit 98 [104: 116: 124: 134: 144: 150: 158: 166] sts evenly all round armhole edge.
Cast off knitwise (on **WS**).
See information page for finishing instructions.

SMIRK

SIZE

To fit bust (cm/in)

71-76	81-86	91-97	102-107	112-117	122-127	132-137	142-147	152-157
28-30	32-34	36-38	40-42	44-46	48-50	52-54	56-58	60-62

Actual bust measurement of garment

90	101	110	121	130	141	150	161	172
35½	39¾	43¼	47¾	51¼	55½	59	63½	67¾

YARN | Summerlite DK and Kidsilk Haze

A Summerlite DK (50gm) Silvery Blue 468

13	14	15	16	18	19	20	22	23

B Kidsilk Haze (25gm) Aura 676

8	9	9	10	11	12	13	14	14

NEEDLES

1 pair 3¾mm (no 9) (US 5) needles
3¾mm (no 9) (US 5) circular needle (no shorter than 100 cm)

EXTRAS

Stitch holders

BUTTONS - 3

TENSION

18 sts and 48 rows to 10 cm / 4 in measured over patt using 3¾mm (US 5) needles and one strand each of yarns A and B held together.

SPECIAL ABBREVIATION

K1 below = K into next st one row below and slip st above off at same time.

BACK

Using 3¾mm (US 5) needles and one strand each of yarns A and B held together cast on 81 [91: 99: 109: 117: 127: 135: 145: 155] sts.
Foundation row (WS): K1, *P1, K1, rep from * to end.
Now work in patt as folls:
Row 1 (RS): K1, *K1 below (see special abbreviation), P1, rep from * to last 2 sts, K1 below (see special abbreviation), K1.
Row 2 (WS): K1, *P1, K1 below (see special abbreviation), rep from * to last 2 sts, P1, K1.
These 2 rows form patt.
Cont in patt until back meas 60 [62: 64: 66: 68: 70: 71: 73: 74] cm, ending with RS facing for next row.
Shape shoulders and back neck
Next row (RS): Cast off 6 [7: 9: 10: 11: 13: 14: 16: 18] sts, patt until there are 15 [16: 20: 23: 26: 28: 31: 34: 38] sts on right needle and turn, leaving rem sts on a holder.
Work each side of neck separately.
Keeping patt correct, dec 1 st at neck edge of next 3 rows, ending with RS facing for next row, **and at same time** cast off 6 [7: 9: 10: 11: 13: 14: 16: 18] sts at beg of 2nd row.
Cast off rem 6 [6: 8: 10: 12: 12: 14: 15: 17] sts.
Return to sts left on holder and slip centre 39 [45: 41: 43: 43: 45: 45: 45: 45] sts onto another holder (for front band).
Rejoin yarn with RS facing and patt to end. Complete to match first side, reversing shapings.

POCKET LININGS (make 2)

Using 3¾mm (US 5) needles and one strand each of yarns A and B held together cast on 23 [23: 23: 25: 25: 25: 27: 27: 27] sts.
Work foundation row as given for back.
Beg with patt row 1, now work in patt as given for back for 60 [64: 64: 68: 68: 72: 72: 76: 76] rows, ending with RS facing for next row.
Break yarn and leave sts on a holder.

LEFT FRONT

Using 3¾mm (US 5) needles and one strand each of yarns A and B held together cast on 37 [41: 45: 51: 55: 59: 63: 69: 73] sts.
Work foundation row as given for back.
Beg with patt row 1, now work in patt as given for back throughout as folls:
Work 72 [76: 76: 80: 80: 84: 84: 88: 88] rows, ending with RS facing for next row. **

Place pocket
Next row (RS): Patt 4 [6: 8: 8: 10: 12: 12: 14: 16] sts, slip next 23 [23: 23: 25: 25: 25: 27: 27: 27] sts onto a holder and, in their place, patt across 23 [23: 23: 25: 25: 25: 27: 27: 27] sts of first pocket lining, patt rem 10 [12: 14: 18: 20: 22: 24: 28 30] sts.
Cont in patt until left front meas 35 [37: 39: 40: 42: 43: 44: 46: 46] cm, ending with RS facing for next row.

Shape front slope

Keeping patt correct, dec 1 st at end of next and 2 [2: 2: 5: 5: 3: 3: 6: 0] foll 4th rows, then on 16 [16: 16: 15: 15: 17: 17: 15: 19] foll 6th rows. 18 [22: 26: 30: 34: 38: 42: 47: 53] sts.
Cont straight until left front matches back to beg of shoulder shaping, ending with RS facing for next row.

Shape shoulder

Keeping patt correct, cast off 6 [7: 9: 10: 11: 13: 14: 16: 18] sts at beg of next and foll alt row.
Work 1 row.
Cast off rem 6 [6: 8: 10: 12: 12: 14: 15: 17] sts.

RIGHT FRONT

Work as give for left front to **.

Place pocket

Next row (RS): Patt 10 [12: 14: 18: 20: 22: 24: 28 30] sts, slip next 23 [23: 23: 25: 25: 25: 27: 27: 27] sts onto a holder and, in their place, patt across 23 [23: 23: 25: 25: 25: 27: 27: 27] sts of second pocket lining, patt rem 4 [6: 8: 8: 10: 12: 12: 14: 16] sts.
Complete to match left front, reversing shapings.

SLEEVES

Using 3¾mm (US 5) needles and one strand each of yarns A and B held together cast on 43 [45: 47: 49: 49: 51: 51: 53: 53] sts.
Work foundation row as given for back.
Beg with patt row 1, now work in patt as given for back throughout as folls:
Work 16 rows, ending with RS facing for next row.
Inc 1 st at each end of next and every foll 8th [8th: 6th: 6th: 6th: 6th: 4th: 4th: 4th] row to 67 [75: 57: 63: 87: 105: 59: 67: 79] sts, then on every foll 10th [10th: 8th: 8th: 8th: -: 6th: 6th: 6th] row until there are 79 [83: 89: 93: 99: -: 107: 111: 115] sts, taking inc sts into patt.
Cont straight until sleeve meas 39 [40: 40: 41: 41: 41: 41: 41: 41] cm, ending with RS facing for next row.
Cast off.

MAKING UP

Press as described on the information page.
Join both shoulder seams.

Front band

With RS facing, using 3¾mm (US 5) circular needle and one strand each of yarns A and B held together, beg and ending at front cast-on edges, pick up and knit 77 [81: 85: 87: 91: 93: 97: 101: 101] sts up right front opening edge to beg of front slope shaping, 63 [63: 63: 65: 65: 67: 67: 67: 69] sts up right front slope, and 3 sts down right back neck slope, K across 39 [41: 41: 43: 43: 45: 45: 45: 45] sts on back holder, then pick up and knit 3 sts up left side of back neck, 63 [63: 63: 65: 65: 67: 67: 67: 69] sts down left front slope to beg of front slope shaping, and 77 [81: 85: 87: 91: 93: 97: 101: 101] sts down left front opening edge. 325 [339: 343: 353: 361: 371: 379: 387: 391] sts.
Row 1 (WS): K1, *P1, K1, rep from * to end.
Row 2: K2, *P1, K1, rep from * to last st, K1.
These 2 rows form rib.
Cont in rib until band meas 4 cm from pick-up row, ending with RS facing for next row.
Next row (RS): Rib 4, *cast off 2 sts (to make a buttonhole – cast on 2 sts over these cast-off sts on next row), rib until there are 33 [35: 37: 38: 40: 41: 43: 45: 45] sts on right needle after cast-off, rep from * once more, cast off 2 sts (to make 3rd buttonhole – cast on 2 sts over these cast-off sts on next row), rib to end.
Cont in rib until band meas 8 cm from pick-up row, ending with RS facing for next row.
Cast off in rib.

Pocket tops (both alike)

Slip 23 [23: 23: 25: 25: 25: 27: 27: 27] sts from pocket holder onto 3¾mm (US 5) needle.
Rejoin one strand each of yarns A and B held together with RS facing and, beg with row 2, work in rib as given for front band for 3 rows, ending with **WS** facing for next row.
Cast off in rib (on **WS**).
Join cast on edges of picket linings to WS of Left and Right Fronts.
Mark points along side seam edges 23 [24: 25.5: 27: 28.5: 30: 31: 32: 33] cm either side of shoulder seams (to denote base of armhole openings). See information page for finishing instructions, setting in sleeves using the straight cast-off method.

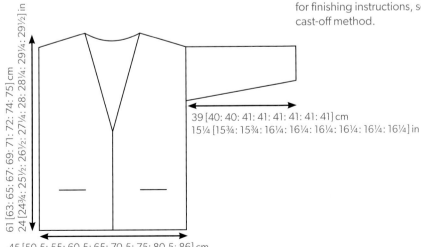

61 [63: 65: 67: 69: 71: 72: 74: 75] cm
24 [24¾: 25½: 26½: 27¼: 28: 28¼: 29¼: 29½] in

39 [40: 40: 41: 41: 41: 41: 41: 41] cm
15¼ [15¾: 15¾: 16¼: 16¼: 16¼: 16¼: 16¼: 16¼] in

45 [50.5: 55: 60.5: 65: 70.5: 75: 80.5: 86] cm
17¾ [20: 21¾: 23¾: 25½: 27¾: 29½: 31¾: 33¾] in

PERIWINKLE

DESIGNED BY
quail studio

SIZE

To fit bust (cm/in)

71-76	81-86	91-97	102-107	112-117	122-127	132-137	142-147	152-157
28-30	32-34	36-38	40-42	44-46	48-50	52-54	56-58	60-62

Actual bust measurement of garment

102	111	119	131	140	153	161	169	182
40¼	43¾	46¾	51½	55	60¼	63½	66½	71¾

YARN | Handknit Cotton (50gm)

10	10	11	11	11	12	12	12	13

(photographed in Cloud 345)

NEEDLES

1 pair 4½mm (no 7) (US 7) needles
1 pair 5mm (no 6) (US 8) needles
4½mm (no 7) (US 7) circular needle no shorter than 100 cm

EXTRA

Stitch holder

TENSION

19 sts and 20 rows to 10 cm / 4 in measured over patt using 5mm (US 8) needles.

BACK

Hem border
Using 4½mm (US 7) needles cast on 10 sts.
Work in g st until this strip, when very slightly stretched, meas 51 [55: 59.5: 65.5: 70: 76.5: 80.5: 84.5: 91] cm, ending with RS facing for next row.
Cast off but do NOT break yarn.

Main section
With RS facing and using 5mm (US 8) needles, pick up and knit 97 [105: 113: 125: 133: 145: 153: 161: 173] sts evenly along row-end edge of hem border.
Now work in patt as folls:
Rows 1 to 3: Knit.
Row 4 (RS): K1, *yfrn, P3tog, yon, K1, rep from * to end.
Row 5 (WS): P2tog, yon, K1, *yfrn, P3tog, yon, K1, rep from * to last 2 sts, yfrn, P2tog.
Rows 6 to 23: As rows 4 and 5, 9 times.
Row 24 (WS): Knit.
These 24 rows form patt.
Cont in patt until back meas 54 [54: 54: 66: 66: 66: 66: 66: 66] cm **from lower edge of hem border**, ending after patt row 3 and with RS facing for next row.

Shape shoulders
Next row (RS): Cast off 35 [39: 43: 47: 51: 57: 61: 65: 71] sts, K until there are 27 [27: 27: 31: 31: 31: 31: 31: 31] sts on right needle and slip these sts onto a holder (for front band), cast off rem 35 [39: 43: 47: 51: 57: 61: 65: 71] sts.

LEFT FRONT

Hem border
Using 4½mm (US 7) needles cast on 10 sts.
Work in g st until this strip, when very slightly stretched, meas 18 [20.5: 22.5: 24.5: 26.5: 30: 32: 34: 37] cm, ending with RS facing for next row.
Cast off but do NOT break yarn.

Main section
With RS facing and using 5mm (US 8) needles, pick up and knit 35 [39: 43: 47: 51: 57: 61: 65: 71] sts evenly along row-end edge of hem border.
Now work in patt as folls:
Rows 1 to 3: Knit.
Row 4 (RS): K1, *yfrn, P3tog, yon, K1, rep from * to 2 [2: 2: 2: 2: 0: 0: 0: 2] sts, (yfrn, P2tog) 1 [1: 1: 1: 1: 0: 0: 0: 1] times.
Row 5 (WS): (P2tog, yon) 0 [0: 0: 0: 0: 1: 1: 1: 0] times, K1, *yfrn, P3tog, yon, K1, rep from * to last 2 sts, yfrn, P2tog.
Rows 6 to 23: As rows 4 and 5, 9 times.
Row 24 (WS): Knit.
These 24 rows form patt.
Cont in patt until left front matches back to shoulder cast-off, ending with RS facing for next row.

Shape shoulder
Cast off all 35 [39: 43: 47: 51: 57: 61: 65: 71] sts.

RIGHT FRONT

Hem border
Work as given for hem border of left front.

Main section
With RS facing and using 5mm (US 8) needles, pick up and knit 35 [39: 43: 47: 51: 57: 61: 65: 71] sts evenly along row-end edge of hem border.

Now work in patt as folls:
Rows 1 to 3: Knit.
Row 4 (RS): (P2tog, yon) 1 [1: 1: 1: 1: 0: 0: 0: 1] times, K1, *yfrn, P3tog, yon, K1, rep from * to end.
Row 5 (WS): P2tog, yon, K1, *yfrn, P3tog, yon, K1, rep from * to last 0 [0: 0: 0: 0: 2: 2: 2: 0] sts, (yfrn, P2tog) 0 [0: 0: 0: 0: 1: 1: 1: 0] times.
Rows 6 to 23: As rows 4 and 5, 9 times.
Row 24 (WS): Knit.
These 24 rows form patt.
Complete to match left front.

SLEEVES
Cuff border
Using 4½mm (US 7) needles cast on 10 sts.
Work in g st until this strip, when very slightly stretched, meas 32 [34: 38: 40: 44.5: 46.5: 48.5: 51: 50.5] cm, ending with RS facing for next row.
Cast off but do NOT break yarn.
Main section
With RS facing and using 5mm (US 8) needles, pick up and knit 61 [65: 73: 77: 85: 89: 93: 97: 101] sts evenly along row-end edge of cuff border.
Beg with row 1, work in patt as given for back until sleeve meas 42 cm **from lower edge of cuff border**, ending after patt row 3 and with RS facing for next row.
Cast off.

MAKING UP
Press as described on the information page.
Join both shoulder seams.
Front band
With RS facing and using 4½mm (US 7) circular needle, beg and ending at lower edges of front hem borders, pick up and knit 107 [107: 107: 128: 128: 128: 128: 128: 128] sts up entire right front opening edge, K across 27 [27: 27: 31: 31: 31: 31: 31: 31] sts on back holder, then pick up and knit 107 [107: 107: 128: 128: 128: 128: 128: 128] sts down entire left front opening edge. 241 [241: 241: 287: 287: 287: 287: 287: 287] sts.
Work in g st for 5 cm, ending with **WS** facing for next row.
Cast off knitwise (on **WS**).
Mark points along side seam edges 17 [18: 19.5: 21: 22.5: 24: 25: 26: 27] cm either side of shoulder seams (to denote base of armhole openings). See information page for finishing instructions, setting in sleeves using the straight cast-off method.

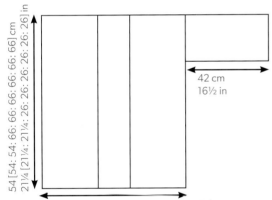

54 [54: 54: 66: 66: 66: 66: 66: 66] cm
21¼ [21¼: 21¼: 26: 26: 26: 26: 26: 26] in

42 cm
16½ in

51 [55.5: 59.5: 65.5: 70: 76.5: 80.5: 84.5: 91] cm
20 [21¾: 23½: 25¾: 27½: 30: 31¾: 33¼: 35¾] in

BLUSHES

SIZE
To fit bust (cm/in)

71-76	81-86	91-97	102-107	112-117	122-127	132-137	142-147	152-157
28-30	32-34	36-38	40-42	44-46	48-50	52-54	56-58	60-62

Actual bust measurement of garment

81	92	101	112	121	132	141	152	162.5
32	36¼	39¾	44	47¾	52	55½	59¾	64

YARN | Summerlite DK (50gm)

9	9	10	10	11	11	12	12	13

(photographed in Pink Powder 472)

NEEDLES
1 pair 3¼mm (no 10) (US 3) needles
1 pair 3¾mm (no 9) (US 5) needles
3¼mm (no 10) (US 3) circular needle no shorter than 100 cm

EXTRAS
Stitch holders

BUTTONS - 3

TENSION
22 sts and 30 rows to 10 cm / 4 in measured over patt using 3¾mm (US 5) needles.

SPECIAL ABBREVIATION
MB = make bobble as folls: K into front, back, front, back and front again of next st, (do NOT turn but slip these 5 sts back onto left needle, K5) 3 times, lift 2nd, 3rd, 4th and 5th st on right needle over first st and off right needle.

BACK
Using 3¼mm (US 3) needles cast on 89 [101: 111: 123: 133: 145: 155: 167: 179] sts.
Row 1 (RS): K1, *P1, K1, rep from * to end.
Row 2 (WS): P1, *K1, P1, rep from * to end.
These 2 rows form rib.
Cont in rib until back meas 8 cm, ending with RS facing for next row.
Change to 3¾mm (US 5) needles.
Now work in patt as folls:
Row 1 (RS): Knit.
Row 2: Purl.
Rows 3 to 6: As rows 1 and 2, twice.
Row 7: K8 [2: 7: 1: 6: 12: 5: 11: 5], MB, *K11, MB, rep from * to last 8 [2: 7: 1: 6: 12: 5: 11: 5] sts, K8 [2: 7: 1: 6: 12: 5: 11: 5].
Row 8: Purl.
Rows 9 to 14: As rows 1 and 2, 3 times.
Row 15: K2 [8: 1: 7: 12: 6: 11: 5: 11], MB, *K11, MB, rep from * to last 2 [8: 1: 7: 12: 6: 11: 5: 11] sts, K2 [8: 1: 7: 12: 6: 11: 5: 11].
Row 16: Purl.
These 16 rows form patt.
Cont in patt until back meas approx 29.5 [30.5: 31: 31.5: 32: 32.5: 32.5: 33.5: 33.5] cm, ending 1 [5: 7: 7: 1: 3: 3: 5: 5] rows after a bobble row and with RS facing for next row.

Shape armholes
Keeping patt correct throughout, cast off 3 [4: 5: 6: 7: 8: 9: 10: 11] sts at beg of next 2 rows. 83 [93: 101: 111: 119: 129: 137: 147: 157] sts.
Dec 1 st at each end of next 3 [5: 5: 7: 7: 7: 9: 11: 11] rows, then on foll 2 [3: 4: 4: 5: 6: 6: 8: 11] alt rows, then on foll 4th row. 71 [75: 81: 87: 93: 101: 105: 107: 111] sts.
Cont straight until armhole meas 18 [19: 20.5: 22: 23.5: 25: 26: 27: 28] cm, ending with RS facing for next row.

Shape shoulders and back neck
Next row (RS): Cast off 9 [9: 11: 12: 13: 15: 16: 16: 17] sts, patt until there are 13 [14: 15: 16: 18: 19: 20: 21: 22] sts on right needle and turn, leaving rem sts on a holder.
Work each side of neck separately.
Cast off 4 sts at beg of next row.
Cast off rem 9 [10: 11: 12: 14: 15: 16: 17: 18] sts.
Return to sts left on holder and slip centre 27 [29: 29: 31: 31: 33: 33: 33: 33] sts onto another holder (for front band).
Rejoin yarn with RS facing and patt to end. Complete to match first side, reversing shapings.

LEFT FRONT
Using 3¼mm (US 3) needles cast on 38 [44: 48: 54: 60: 66: 70: 76: 82] sts.
Row 1 (RS): *K1, P1, rep from * to last 2 sts, K2.
Row 2 (WS): *K1, P1, rep from * to end.
These 2 rows form rib.
Cont in rib until left front meas 8 cm, inc 0 [0: 1: 1: 0: 0: 1: 1: 1] st at end of last row and ending with RS facing for next row. 38 [44: 49: 55: 60: 66: 71: 77: 83] sts.
Change to 3¾mm (US 5) needles.

Now work in patt as folls:
Row 1 (RS): Knit.
Row 2: Purl.
Rows 3 to 6: As rows 1 and 2, twice.
Row 7: K8 [2: 7: 1: 6: 12: 5: 11: 5], MB, *K11, MB, rep from * to last 5 sts, K5.
Row 8: Purl.
Rows 9 to 14: As rows 1 and 2, 3 times.
Row 15: K2 [8: 1: 7: 12: 6: 11: 5: 11], *MB, K11, rep from * to end.
Row 16: Purl.
These 16 rows form patt.
Cont in patt until 18 rows less have been worked than on back to beg of armhole shaping, ending 7 [3: 5: 5: 7: 1: 1: 3: 3] rows after a bobble row and with RS facing for next row.
Shape front slope
Keeping patt correct throughout, dec 1 st at end of next and 2 foll 6th rows. 35 [41: 46: 52: 57: 63: 68: 74: 80] sts.
Work 5 rows, ending with RS facing for next row.
Shape armhole
Keeping patt correct throughout, cast off 3 [4: 5: 6: 7: 8: 9: 10: 11] sts at beg and dec 1 st at end of next row. 31 [36: 40: 45: 49: 54: 58: 63: 68] sts.
Work 1 row.
Dec 1 st at front slope edge of 5th and 5 [7: 5: 7: 5: 6: 5: 3: 2] foll 6th rows, then on 1 [0: 2: 1: 3: 3: 4: 6: 7] foll 8th rows **and at same time** dec 1 st at armhole edge of next 3 [5: 5: 7: 7: 7: 9: 11: 11] rows, then on foll 2 [3: 4: 4: 5: 6: 6: 8: 11] alt rows, then on foll 4th row. 18 [19: 22: 24: 27: 30: 32: 33: 35] sts.
Cont straight until left front matches back to beg of shoulder shaping.
Shape shoulder
Cast off 9 [9: 11: 12: 13: 15: 16: 16: 17] sts at beg of next row.
Work 1 row.
Cast off rem 9 [10: 11: 12: 14: 15: 16: 17: 18] sts.

RIGHT FRONT
Using 3¼mm (US 3) needles cast on 38 [44: 48: 54: 60: 66: 70: 76: 82] sts.
Row 1 (RS): K2, *P1, K1, rep from * to end.
Row 2 (WS): *P1, K1, rep from * to end.
These 2 rows form rib.
Cont in rib until right front meas 8 cm, inc 0 [0: 1: 1: 0: 0: 1: 1: 1] st at beg of last row and ending with RS facing for next row. 38 [44: 49: 55: 60: 66: 71: 77: 83] sts.
Change to 3¾mm (US 5) needles.
Now work in patt as folls:
Row 1 (RS): Knit.
Row 2: Purl.
Rows 3 to 6: As rows 1 and 2, twice.
Row 7: K5, MB, *K11, MB, rep from * to last 8 [2: 7: 1: 6: 12: 5: 11: 5] sts, K8 [2: 7: 1: 6: 12: 5: 11: 5].
Row 8: Purl.
Rows 9 to 14: As rows 1 and 2, 3 times.
Row 15: *K11, MB, rep from * to last 2 [8: 1: 7: 12: 6: 11: 5: 11] sts, K2 [8: 1: 7: 12: 6: 11: 5: 11].
Row 16: Purl.
These 16 rows form patt.

Cont in patt until 18 rows less have been worked than on back to beg of armhole shaping, ending 7 [3: 5: 5: 7: 1: 1: 3: 3] rows after a bobble row and with RS facing for next row.
Shape front slope
Keeping patt correct throughout, dec 1 st at beg of next and 2 foll 6th rows. 35 [41: 46: 52: 57: 63: 68: 74: 80] sts.
Work 4 rows, ending with **WS** facing for next row.
Complete to match left front, reversing shapings.

SLEEVES
Using 3¼mm (US 3) needles cast on 41 [45: 47: 49: 49: 51: 51: 53: 53] sts.
Work in rib as given for back for 10 cm, ending with RS facing for next row.
Change to 3¾mm (US 5) needles.
Next row (RS): K3 [0: 1: 2: 2: 3: 3: 4: 4], inc in next st, (K2 [3: 3: 3: 3: 3: 3: 3: 3], inc in next st) 11 times, K4 [0: 1: 2: 2: 3: 3: 4: 4]. 53 [57: 59: 61: 61: 63: 63: 65: 65] sts.
Beg with a **purl** row, work in st st for 3 [1: 7: 3: 1: 7: 7: 5: 5] rows, inc 1 [0: 1: 1: 0: 1: 1: 1: 1] st at each end of 2nd [-: 2nd: 2nd: -: 2nd: 2nd: 2nd: 2nd] and foll 0 [-: 2: 0: -: 2: 2: 1: 1] alt rows and ending with RS facing for next row. 55 [57: 65: 63: 61: 69: 69: 69: 69] sts.
Now work in patt as folls:
Row 1 (RS): Inc in first st, K2 [3: 7: 6: 5: 9: 9: 9: 9], MB, *K11, MB, rep from * to last 3 [4: 8: 7: 6: 10: 10: 10: 10] sts, K2 [3: 7: 6: 5: 9: 9: 9: 9], inc in last st. 57 [59: 67: 65: 63: 71: 71: 71: 71] sts.
Beg with a **purl** row, work in st st for 7 rows, inc 1 st at each end of 2nd and foll 2 [2: 1: 2: 2: 1: 2: 2: 2] alt rows. 63 [65: 71: 71: 69: 75: 77: 77: 77] sts.
Row 9 (RS): Inc in first st, K0 [1: 4: 3: 6: 7: 7: 7], MB, *K11, MB, rep from * to last 1 [2: 5: 5: 4: 7: 8: 8: 8] sts, K0 [1: 4: 3: 6: 7: 7: 7], inc in last st. 65 [67: 73: 73: 71: 77: 79: 79: 79] sts.
Beg with a **purl** row, work in st st for 7 rows, inc 1 st at each end of 4th [2nd: 2nd: 4th: 2nd: 4th: 4th: 2nd: 2nd] and foll 0 [0: 1: 0: 0: 0: 0: 0: 2] alt rows, then on 0 [1: 0: 0: 1: 0: 0: 1: 0] foll 4th row. 67 [71: 77: 75: 75: 79: 81: 83: 85] sts.
Last 16 rows form patt and beg sleeve shaping.
Cont in patt, shaping sides by inc 1 st at each end of 21st [21st: 7th: 5th: 3rd: next: next: 3rd: next] and foll 0 [0: 0: 0: 0: 0: 0: 0: 1] foll alt row, then on 0 [0: 0: 0: 0: 2: 7: 9: 9: 9] foll 4th rows, then on 0 [0: 0: 0: 5: 1: 0: 0: 0] foll 6th rows, then on 0 [0: 0: 4: 0: 0: 0: 0: 0] foll 8th rows, taking inc sts into patt. 69 [73: 79: 85: 91: 97: 101: 103: 107] sts.
Cont straight until sleeve meas approx 33 [34: 34: 35: 35: 35: 35: 35: 35] cm, ending 1 [5: 7: 7: 1: 3: 3: 5: 5] rows after a bobble row and with RS facing for next row.
Shape top
Keeping patt correct, cast off 3 [4: 5: 6: 7: 8: 9: 10: 11] sts at beg of next 2 rows. 63 [65: 69: 73: 77: 81: 83: 83: 85] sts.
Dec 1 st at each end of next and foll 2 alt rows, then on 2 foll 4th rows. 53 [55: 59: 63: 67: 71: 73: 73: 75] sts.
Work 1 row.
Dec 1 st at each end of next and foll 3 [4: 4: 4: 4: 4: 5: 7: 8] alt rows, then on foll 7 [7: 9: 11: 13: 15: 15: 13: 13] rows, ending with RS facing for next row. 31 sts.
Cast off 3 sts at beg of next 4 rows.
Cast off rem 19 sts.

MAKING UP

Press as described on the information page.

Join both shoulder seams.

Front band

With RS facing and using 3¼mm (US 3) circular needle, beg and ending at front cast-on edges, pick up and knit 55 [57: 59: 61: 61: 63: 63: 65: 65] sts up right front opening edge to beg of front slope shaping, 58 [61: 64: 68: 71: 75: 77: 80: 82] sts up right front slope, and 3 sts down right back neck slope, K across 27 [29: 29: 31: 31: 33: 33: 33: 33] sts on back holder, then pick up and knit 3 sts up left side of back neck, 58 [61: 64: 68: 71: 75: 77: 80: 82] sts down left front slope to beg of front slope shaping, and 55 [57: 59: 61: 61: 63: 63: 65: 65] sts down left front opening edge. 259 [271: 281: 295: 301: 315: 319: 329: 333] sts.

Row 1 (WS): K1, *P1, K1, rep from * to end.

Row 2 (RS): K2, *P1, K1, rep from * to last st, K1.

These 2 rows form rib.

Cont in rib for a further 9 rows, ending with RS facing for next row.

Row 12 (RS): Rib 4, *cast off 2 sts (to make a buttonhole – cast on 2 sts over these cast-off sts on next row), rib until there are 22 [23: 24: 25: 25: 26: 26: 27: 27] sts on right needle after cast-off, rep from * once more, cast off 2 sts (to make 3rd buttonhole – cast on 2 sts over these cast-off sts on next row), rib to end.

Work in rib for a further 13 rows, ending with RS facing for next row.

Cast off in rib.

Mark points along side seam edges 18 [19: 20.5: 22: 23.5: 25: 26: 27: 28] cm either side of shoulder seams (to denote base of armhole openings). See information page for finishing instructions, setting in sleeves using the set-in method.

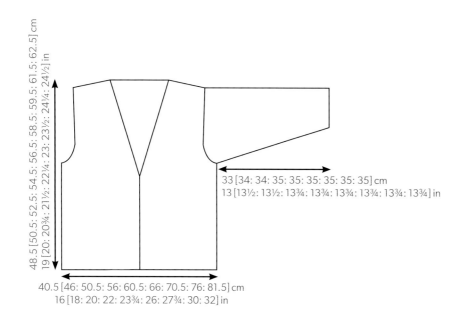

48.5 [50.5: 52.5: 54.5: 56.5: 58.5: 59.5: 61.5: 62.5] cm
19 [20: 20¾: 21½: 22¼: 23: 23½: 24¼: 24½] in

33 [34: 34: 35: 35: 35: 35: 35: 35] cm
13 [13½: 13½: 13¾: 13¾: 13¾: 13¾: 13¾: 13¾] in

40.5 [46: 50.5: 56: 60.5: 66: 70.5: 76: 81.5] cm
16 [18: 20: 22: 23¾: 26: 27¾: 30: 32] in

FLORA

SIZE

To fit bust (cm/in)

71-76	81-86	91-97	102-107	112-117	122-127	132-137	142-147	152-157
28-30	32-34	36-38	40-42	44-46	48-50	52-54	56-58	60-62

Actual bust measurement of garment

85	96	106	117	125	136	146	157	167
33½	37¾	41¾	46	49¼	53½	57½	61¾	65¾

YARN | Handknit Cotton (50gm)

11	11	12	12	13	13	14	14	15

(photographed in Ballet Pink 372)

NEEDLES

1 pair 3½mm (no 9/10) (US 4) needles
1 pair 4mm (no 8) (US 6) needles
3½mm (no 9/10) (US 4) circular needle no shorter than 120 cm

EXTRA

Stitch holder

TENSION

19 sts and 28 rows to 10 cm / 4 in measured over patt using 4mm (US 6) needles.

BACK

Using 3½mm (US 4) needles cast on 81 [91: 101: 111: 119: 129: 139: 149: 159] sts.
Row 1 (RS): K1, *P1, K1, rep from * to end.
Row 2 (WS): P1, *K1, P1, rep from * to end.
These 2 rows form rib.
Cont in rib for a further 10 rows, ending with RS facing for next row.
Change to 4mm (US 6) needles.
Beg with a K row, now work in st st for 2 rows, ending with RS facing for next row.
Now work in patt as folls:
Row 1 (RS): Knit.
Row 2 (WS): Purl.
Row 3: K1 [3: 2: 1: 2: 1: 3: 2: 1], yfwd, K2tog, *K1, yfwd, K2tog, rep from * to last 0 [2: 1: 0: 1: 0: 2: 1: 0] sts, K0 [2: 1: 0: 1: 0: 2: 1: 0].
Row 4: Purl.
These 4 rows form patt.
Cont in patt until back meas 58 [60: 62: 64: 66: 68: 69: 71: 72] cm, ending with RS facing for back neck.
Shape shoulders and back neck
Next row (RS): Cast off 6 [7: 8: 9: 10: 11: 12: 13: 15] sts, patt until there are 22 [25: 29: 32: 35: 38: 42: 46: 49] sts on right needle and turn, leaving rem sts on a holder.
Work each side of neck separately.
Keeping patt correct throughout, dec 1 st at neck edge of next 4 rows **and at same time** cast off 6 [7: 8: 9: 10: 11: 12: 14: 15] sts at beg of 2nd row, then 6 [7: 8: 9: 10: 11: 13: 14: 15] sts at beg of foll alt row.
Work 1 row.

Cast off rem 6 [7: 9: 10: 11: 12: 13: 14: 15] sts.
Return to sts left on holder and slip centre 25 [27: 27: 29: 29: 31: 31: 31: 31] sts onto another holder (for front band).
Rejoin yarn with RS facing and patt to end. Complete to match first side, reversing shapings.

LEFT FRONT

Using 3½mm (US 4) needles cast on 34 [38: 44: 48: 52: 58: 62: 68: 72] sts.
Row 1 (RS): *K1, P1, rep from * to last 2 sts, K2.
Row 2 (WS): *K1, P1, rep from * to end.
These 2 rows form rib.
Cont in rib for a further 10 rows, inc 0 [1: 0: 1: 0: 1: 0: 1] st at end of last row and ending with RS facing for next row. 34 [39: 44: 49: 53: 58: 63: 68: 73] sts.
Change to 4mm (US 6) needles.
Beg with a K row, now work in st st for 2 rows, ending with RS facing for next row.
Now work in patt as folls:
Row 1 (RS): Knit.
Row 2: Purl.
Row 3: K1 [3: 2: 1: 2: 1: 3: 2: 1], yfwd, K2tog, *K1, yfwd, K2tog, rep from * to last st, K1.
Row 4: Purl.
These 4 rows form patt.
Cont in patt until 78 [78: 78: 80: 80: 84: 84: 84: 86] rows less have been worked than on back to beg of shoulder shaping, ending with RS facing for next row.
Shape front slope
Keeping patt correct, dec 1 st at end of next and 1 [5: 5: 8: 8: 10: 10: 10: 9] foll 6th rows, then on 8 [5: 5: 3: 3: 2: 2: 2: 3] foll 8th rows. 24 [28: 33: 37: 41: 45: 50: 55: 60] sts.
Work 7 rows, ending with RS facing for next row.

Shape shoulder

Cast off 6 [7: 8: 9: 10: 11: 12: 13: 15] sts at beg of next and foll 2 [2: 2: 2: 2: 2: 1: 0: 2] alt rows. then 0 [0: 0: 0: 0: 0: 13: 14: 0] sts at beg of foll – [-: -: -: -: -: 1: 2: -] alt rows.
Work 1 row.
Cast off rem 6 [7: 9: 10: 11: 12: 13: 14: 15] sts.

RIGHT FRONT

Using 3½mm (US 4) needles cast on 34 [38: 44: 48: 52: 58: 62: 68: 72] sts.
Row 1 (RS): K2, *P1, K1, rep from * to end.
Row 2 (WS): *P1, K1, rep from * to end.
These 2 rows form rib.
Cont in rib for a further 10 rows, inc 0 [1: 0: 1: 1: 0: 1: 0: 1] st at beg of last row and ending with RS facing for next row. 34 [39: 44: 49: 53: 58: 63: 68: 73] sts.
Change to 4mm (US 6) needles.
Beg with a K row, now work in st st for 2 rows, ending with RS facing for next row.
Now work in patt as folls:
Row 1 (RS): Knit.
Row 2 (WS): Purl.
Row 3: K2, yfwd, K2tog, *K1, yfwd, K2tog, rep from * to last 0 [2: 1: 0: 1: 0: 2: 1: 0] sts, K0 [2: 1: 0: 1: 0: 2: 1: 0].
Row 4: Purl.
These 4 rows form patt.
Complete to match left front, reversing shapings.

SLEEVES

Using 3½mm (US 4) needles cast on 37 [39: 41: 43: 43: 45: 45: 47: 47] sts.
Work in rib as given for back for 12 rows, ending with RS facing for next row.
Change to 4mm (US 6) needles.
Beg with a K row, now work in st st for 2 rows, inc 1 st at each end of both rows and ending with RS facing for next row. 41 [43: 45: 47: 47: 49: 49: 51: 51] sts.
Now work in patt as folls:
Row 1 (RS): Inc in first st, K to last st, inc in last st. 43 [45: 47: 49: 49: 51: 51: 53: 53] sts.
Row 2 (WS): Inc in first st, P to last st, inc in last st. 45 [47: 49: 51: 51: 53: 53: 55: 55] sts.

Row 3: Inc in first st, K3 [1: 2: 3: 3: 1: 1: 2: 2], yfwd, K2tog, *K1, yfwd, K2tog, rep from * to last 3 [1: 2: 3: 3: 1: 1: 2: 2] sts, K2 [0: 1: 2: 2: 0: 0: 1: 1], inc in last st. 47 [49: 51: 53: 53: 55: 55: 57: 57] sts.
Row 4: As row 2. 49 [51: 53: 55: 55: 57: 57: 59: 59] sts.
These 4 rows form patt and beg sleeve shaping.
Sizes 71-76, 81-86, 91-97, 102-107 only
Cont in patt, shaping sides by inc 1 st at each end of next 10 [10: 12: 14] rows. 69 [71: 77: 83] sts.
Sizes 112-117, 122-127, 132-137, 142-147, 152-157 only
Cont in patt, shaping sides by inc 1 st at each end of next and every alt 16 [18: 19: 21: 22] rows. 89 [95: 97: 103: 105] sts.
Cont without shaping until sleeve meas 47 [46: 46: 45.5: 44: 43.5: 42.5: 42: 40] cm, ending with RS facing for next row.
Cast off.

MAKING UP

Press as described on the information page.
Join both shoulder seams.
Front band
With RS facing and using 3½mm (US 4) circular needle, beg and ending at front cast-on edges, pick up and knit 78 [83: 88: 91: 96: 98: 101: 106: 106] sts up right front opening edge to beg of front slope shaping, 84 [84: 84: 87: 87: 89: 89: 89: 92] sts up right front slope, and 5 sts down right back neck slope, K across 25 [27: 27: 29: 29: 31: 31: 31: 31] sts on back holder, then pick up and knit 5 sts up left side of back neck, 84 [84: 84: 87: 87: 89: 89: 89: 92] sts down left front slope to beg of front slope shaping, and 78 [83: 88: 91: 96: 98: 101: 106: 106] sts down left front opening edge. 359 [371: 381: 395: 405: 415: 421: 431: 437] sts.
Row 1 (WS): K1, *P1, K1, rep from * to end.
Row 2: K2, *P1, K1, rep from * to last st, K1.
These 2 rows form rib.
Cont in rib for a further 9 rows, ending with RS facing for next row.
Cast off in rib.
Mark points along side seam edges 18 [19: 20.5: 22: 23.5: 25: 26: 27: 28] cm either side of shoulder seams (to denote base of armhole openings). See information page for finishing instructions, setting in sleeves using the straight cast-off method.

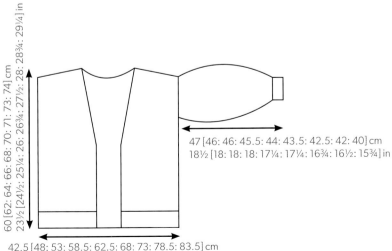

60 [62: 64: 66: 68: 70: 71: 73: 74] cm
23½ [24½: 25¼: 26: 26¾: 27½: 28: 28¾: 29¼] in

47 [46: 46: 45.5: 44: 43.5: 42.5: 42: 40] cm
18½ [18: 18: 18: 17¼: 17¼: 16¾: 16½: 15¾] in

42.5 [48: 53: 58.5: 62.5: 68: 73: 78.5: 83.5] cm
16¾ [19: 20¾: 23: 24½: 26¾: 28¾: 31: 32¾] in

SIZING

We have recently increased our size range to help you achieve the best fit for your knitwear. Our womenswear sizes now range from 28"/71cm through to 62"/157cm across the chest.

Dimensions in the charts below are body measurements, not garment dimensions. Therefore, please refer to the measuring guide to help you to determine which is the best size for you to knit.

STANDARD SIZING GUIDE FOR WOMEN

To fit bust

28-30	32–34	36–38	40–42	44–46	48–50	52-54	56-58	60-62	inches
71–76	81–86	91-97	102–107	112–117	122–127	132-137	142-147	152-157	cm

To fit waist

20-22	24–26	28–30	32–34	36–38	40–42	44-46	48-50	52-54	inches
51-56	61–66	71–76	81–86	91–97	102–107	112-117	122-127	132-137	cm

To fit hips

30-31	34–36	38–40	42–44	46–48	50–52	54-56	58-60	62-64	inches
76-81	86–91	97–102	107–112	117–122	127–132	137-142	147-152	157-162	cm

SIZING & SIZE DIAGRAM NOTE

The instructions are given for the smallest size. Where they vary, work the figures in brackets for the larger sizes. One set of figures refers to all sizes.

Included with most patterns is a size diagram; see image below of the finished garment and its dimensions. The measurement shown at the bottom of each size diagram shows the garment width. The size diagram will also indicate how the garment is constructed. ForZ example, if the garment has a drop shoulder, this will be reflected in the drawing.

To help you choose the size of garment to knit, please refer to the sizing guide. Generally, in the majority of designs, the welt width (at the cast-on edge of the garment) is the same width as the chest.

If you don't want to measure yourself, note the size of a similar shaped garment that you own and compare it with the size diagram given at the end of the pattern.

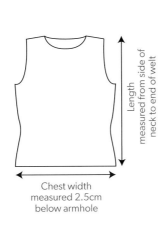
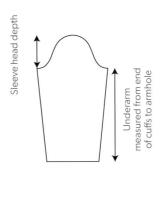

MEASURING GUIDE

For maximum comfort and to ensure the correct fit when choosing a size to knit, please follow the tips below when checking your size. Measure yourself close to your body, over your underwear, and don't pull the tape measure too tight!

Bust/chest | measure around the fullest part of the bust/chest and across the shoulder blades.

Waist | measure around the natural waistline, just above the hip bones.

Hips | measure around the fullest part of the bottom.

The model used in this collection wears a UK dress size 10. Garments were knitted in bust size 32 - 34". Height: 175cm / 5ft 9in

Finally, once you have decided which size is best for you, please ensure that you achieve the tension required for the design you wish to knit.

Remember, if your tension is too loose, your garment will be bigger than the pattern size and you may use more yarn. If your tension is too tight, your garment could be smaller than the pattern size and you will have yarn left over.

Furthermore, if your tension is incorrect, the handle of your fabric will be too stiff or floppy and will not fit properly. It really does make sense to check your tension before starting every project.

TENSION

This is the size of your knitting. Most of the knitting patterns will have a tension quoted. This is how many stitches 10cm/4in in width and how many rows 10cm/4in in length to make a square. If your knitting doesn't match this, then your finished garment will not measure the correct size. To obtain the correct measurements for your garment, you must achieve the tension.

The tension quoted on a ball band is the manufacturer's average. For the manufacturer and designers to produce designs, they have to use a tension for you to be able to obtain the measurements quoted. It's fine not to be the average, but you need to know if you meet the average or not. Then you can make the necessary adjustments to obtain the correct measurements.

CHOOSING YARN

All the colours and textures, where do you start? Look for the thickness - how chunky do you want your finished garment? Sometimes it's colour that draws you to a yarn, or perhaps you have a pattern that requires a specific yarn. Check the washing/care instructions before you buy.

Yarn varies in thickness; there are various descriptions, such as DK and 4ply. These are examples of standard weights. There are a lot of yarns available that are not standard, so it helps to read the ball band to see what the recommended needle size is.

This will give you an idea of the approximate thickness. It is best to use the yarn recommended in the pattern. Keep one ball band from each project so that you have a record of what you have used, and most importantly, how to care for your garment after it has been completed. Always remember to give the ball band with the garment if it is a gift.

The ball band normally provides you with the average tension and recommended needle sizes for the yarn, this may vary from what has been used in the pattern, always go with the pattern as the designer may change needles to obtain a certain look. The ball band also tells you the name of the yarn and what it is made of, the weight and approximate length of the ball of yarn, along with the shade and dye lot numbers. This is important as dye lots can vary, so you need to buy your yarn with matching dye lots.

PRESSING AND AFTERCARE

Having spent so long knitting your project, it can be a great shame not to look after it properly. Some yarns are suitable for pressing once you have finished to improve the look of the fabric. To find out this information, you will need to look on the yarn ball band, where there will be washing and care symbols.

Once you have checked to see if your yarn is suitable to be pressed and the knitting is a smooth texture (stocking stitch, for example), pin out and place a damp cloth onto the knitted pieces. Hold the steam iron (at the correct temperature) approximately 10cm/4in away from the fabric and steam. Keep the knitted pieces pinned in place until cool.

As a test, it is a good idea to wash your tension square in the way you would expect to wash your garment.

EXPERIENCE RATING

(for guidance only)

BEGINNER TECHNIQUES

For the beginner knitter, basic garment shaping and straight forward stitch technique.

SIMPLE TECHNIQUES

Simple straight forward knitting, introducing various shaping techniques and garments.

EXPERIENCED TECHNIQUES

For the more experienced knitter, using more advanced shaping techniques at the same time as colourwork or different stitch techniques.

ADVANCED TECHNIQUES

Advanced techniques used, including advanced stitches and garment shaping.

ABBREVIATIONS

alt	alternate
beg	begin(ning)
cm	centimetres
cont	continue
dec	decrease(s)(ing)
foll(s)	follow(s)(ing)
g	grams
g st	garter stitch (knit all rows)
in	inch(es)
inc	increase(s)(ing)
K	knit
Kfb	knit in front and back of stitch (makes 1 stitch)
M1	make 1 stitch
meas	measures
mm	millimetres
P	purl
patt	pattern
psso	pass slipped stitch over
rem	remain(ing)
rep	repeat
RS	right side of work
Sl 1	slip 1 stitch
st st	stocking stitch (knit on RS rows, purl on WS rows)
st(s)	stitch(es)
tbl	through back of loop
tog	together
WS	wrong side of work